PRAISE FOR Wᴵ‎ᴸᴸᴵᴬᴹ ᴮᴱᴿᴺᴴᴬᴿᴰᵀ

"One of the things I love about these books is that they are so accessible to every aspiring writer."

— RICK LUDWIG, AUTHOR OF *MIRRORED*

"I reread these books before I start each book I write."

— CALLIE HUTTON, *USA TODAY*-BESTSELLING AUTHOR OF *FOR THE LOVE OF THE VISCOUNT*

"Bernhardt shows you exactly what makes literary characters keep people interested and how to use those strengths when creating characters of your own."

— R.J. JOHNSON, AUTHOR OF *THE TWELVE STONES*

"Easy to read while delivering good material with some occasional humor."

— DAVID SULLIVAN, AUTHOR

"This book gives everything that it promises. And all the other writing books written by William Bernhardt are on my wish list."

— C.H. SCARLETT, AUTHOR

DAZZLING DESCRIPTION

Painting the Perfect Picture

WILLIAM BERNHARDT

BABYLON BOOKS

Dedicated to all the Red Sneaker Writers:
You cannot fail if you refuse to quit.

"Don't tell me the moon is shining; show me the glint of light on broken glass."

— ANTON CHEKOV

CONTENTS

INTRODUCTION

If this is not your first Red Sneaker book, or if you've attended Red Sneaker retreats or conventions, you can skip to Chapter One. If you're new, let me take a moment to explain.

I've been telling stories for several decades, doing almost every kind of writing imaginable. I've been speaking at workshops and conferences almost as long. Every time I step behind the podium I see long rows of talented people frustrated by the fact that they haven't sold any books. Yes, the market is changing and agents are hard to find and self-publishing can be challenging. But when aspiring writers work hard but still don't succeed…there's usually a reason. Too often enormous potential is lost due to a lack of fundamental knowledge. Sometimes a little guidance is all that stands between an unknown writer and a satisfying writing career.

I've seen writing instructors and writing texts that seem more interested in appearing literary than in providing useful information. Sometimes I think presenters do more to obfuscate the subject than to explain it. Perhaps they feel that if they make the writing process as mysterious as possible, it will make them seem profound—or perhaps they don't understand the subject well themselves. Some of the best writers I know are not particularly good teachers, because they've never thought consciously about the creative process.

Hoping to be more useful, I founded the Red Sneaker Writing Center. Why Red Sneakers? Because I love my red sneakers. They're practical, flexible, sturdy—full of flair and fun. In other words, they're exactly what writing instruction should be. Practical, dynamic, and designed to unleash the creative spirit, to give the imagination a platform for creating wondrous work.

I held the first Red Sneaker Writers conference in 2005. I invited the best speakers I knew, people who had published many books but also could teach. Then I launched my small-group writing retreats—intensive days working with a handful of aspiring writers. The retreats gave me the opportunity to read, edit, and work one-on-one with people so I could target their needs and make sure they got what would help them most. This approach worked well and I'm proud to say a substantial number of writers have graduated from my programs, published, and even hit the bestseller lists. But of course, not everyone can attend a retreat.

This book, and the others in this series, are designed to provide assistance to writers regardless of their location. The books are short, inexpensive, and targeted to specific areas where a writer might want help.

Let me see if I can anticipate your questions:

Why are these books so short? Because I've expunged the unnecessary and the unhelpful. I've pared it down to the essential information, useful ideas that can improve the quality of your writing. Too many instructional books are padded with excerpts and repetition to fill word counts required by book contracts. That's not the Red Sneaker way.

Why are you writing several different books instead of one big book? I encourage writers to commit to writing every day and to maintain a consistent writing schedule. Sometimes reading about writing can be an excuse for not writing. You can read the Red Sneaker books without losing much time. In fact, each can be read in an afternoon. Take one day off from your writing. Make notes as you read. See if that doesn't trigger ideas about how you might improve your writing. Then get back to work.

You reference other books as examples, but you rarely quote excerpts. Why?

Two reasons. First, I'm trying to keep these books brief. I will cite a book as an example, and if you want to look up a particular passage, it's easy enough to do. You don't need me to cut and paste it for you. Second, if I quote from materials currently under copyright protection, I have to pay a fee, which means I'd need to raise the price of the book. I don't want to do that. I think you can grasp my points without reading copyrighted excerpts. Too often, in my opinion, excessive excerpting is done to pad the page count.

Why does each chapter end with exercises?

The exercises are a completely integrated and essential part of the book, designed to simulate what happens in my small-group writing retreats. Samuel Johnson was correct when he wrote: *Scribendo disces scribere.* Meaning: You learn to write by writing. These principles won't be concretized in your brain until you put them into practice.

So get the full benefit from this book. Complete the exercises. If you were in one of my retreats, this would be your homework. I won't be hovering over your shoulder as you read this book— but you should do the exercises anyway.

What else does the Red Sneaker Writers Center do?

We send out a free e-newsletter filled with writing advice, market analysis, and other items of interest. If you would like to be added to the mailing list, please visit my website. We also have a free bi-weekly Red Sneaker podcast with all the latest news and interviews with industry professionals. I host an annual conference, WriterCon, over Labor Day weekend and small-group writing retreats throughout the year. There will be future books in this series. And we sponsor a literary magazine called *Conclave* that would love to see you submit your poems, short fiction, and creative nonfiction. Our Balkan Press publishes books, primarily fiction and poetry.

Okay, enough of the warm-up act. Read this book. Then write your story. Follow your dreams. Never give up.

William Bernhardt

WHY DESCRIPTION MATTERS

"Try to leave out the part that readers tend to skip."

— ELMORE LEONARD

My admiration for the work of Elmore Leonard is tremendous. He could write every kind of book—western, crime, heist, even satire—and it always turned out well. He had an economic prose style that engaged readers and shaped writers. You can see his influence all over my book on Style, not to mention many modern-day bestsellers, for instance, the work of James Patterson. Short sentences, short paragraphs, short chapters. Never give the reader a chance to become impatient.

But this book is about description, so why am I mentioning this? When asked about his authorial success, Leonard offered a Top Ten list of rules for writing, and as we all know, nothing in the world is so powerful as a Top Ten list. That amalgamation of wisdom has had a profound impact on contemporary writing. For instance, one of the rules lashes out at prologues, and as a result, no one wants to write a prologue anymore. Fool that I am,

I put a prologue at the beginning of all nineteen Ben Kincaid novels. Leonard would not approve. (Just for the record, there's nothing wrong with calling your first chapter a prologue, though there is something wrong with starting your book with a boring chapter that does not launch the story.)

The two items on Leonard's list of most relevance to this book are the ninth and the tenth. In the number nine spot, Leonard addressed description directly. His rule? "Don't go into great detail describing places and things." And why would that be? See Rule #10: "Try to leave out the part that readers tend to skip."

I will point out that Leonard does not say you shouldn't describe anything. He just doesn't want you to rattle on forever about it. How do you know how much you need? How much is enough? I'll discuss that in the next chapter. What I want you to understand now is the unspoken premise lying behind Leonard's rules:

You want readers to read your book, not skim it.

I also want you to understand the necessary corollary, the dangling threat, if you will:

When readers see something that doesn't interest them, they skip it.

Writing the Unskippable

IN A PERFECT WORLD, READERS WOULD NEVER SKIM, NEVER SKIP, would read every word and would enjoy every minute of it. Especially my books. But unfortunately, that's not always the way it works. When readers become antsy, when they see something that looks unpleasant, they skim. If this happens repetitively, they start skipping the offending portions altogether. And eventually, they put down the book and read something else. Or worse, turn on the television and binge-watch something.

Reader engagement is key to reader enjoyment.

I bet you've had the experience of being so involved in a book, so excited about the story or so attached to the characters, that you don't want to put it down and, if possible, read it in a few short gulps. If you can get a reader that attached to your series character, they'll want every book in the series, past or present. If you can get them that wrapped up in your story, they're likely to post on your Amazon page, or on Goodreads, or to tell friends about it. Word of mouth is still the only thing that sells books even if, today, it's typically digital word of mouth. But you only get that if the reader enjoys your book. Yes, I hope they also find it enlightening and uplifting and receive all the valuable take-aways I discussed in the Theme book—but first and foremost, they must enjoy it. Hair-shirt books are for Required Reading lists. When people read for pleasure, they want to an entertaining experience, and if they don't get it they will soon move onto something else.

How do you create reader engagement? Most readers find big blocks of text off-putting. Show them a paragraph that goes on for a page and a half and they'll be skipping and skimming in no time at all. That is never more true than when that endless paragraph is composed of description. Though there are readers who enjoy prosy passages depicting the sunset and such, most have little patience for that sort of thing. This is particularly true in the world of popular fiction, where readers expect a brisk pace and a plot with urgency that compels them to keep turning pages. Excessive description will kill that pace dead. Nothing is worse than a thriller that doesn't thrill, or a romance that doesn't make your heart pound faster. While a little description can be a marvelous tool, too much can become the writer's worst enemy.

Don't let description undermine the pace.

. . .

LEAVING THE DOOR AJAR

ONE OF THE CONTINUING IDEAS OF THIS BOOK WILL BE LEARNING to trust your reader. They do not need everything described for them. They have lived lives of their own and have a stockpile of mental images based upon their own experiences. They can conjure a scene for themselves. While they might require a bit of guidance here and there, they do not want endless descriptions of the commonplace, and if you insist on writing that, it will not be long before you lose them. If you are describing the less commonplace, more words may be advisable. But in no case do readers need every little detail spelled out. They have imaginations. That's why they like books. Focus instead on what readers can't create for themselves—like sparkling characters, ingenious plots, and a rapid pace.

Description matters enough that I'm devoting an entire book to it. You can't avoid it, every book must have some—and yet, mishandled, it can be lethal to your success. On a more positive note, handled well, description can create admiration and appreciation. So let's make sure you do it well. This is your chance to dazzle the reader. This is your chance to blow their minds—not put them to sleep.

Description matters.

As they embark on a new book, readers understand there will be a learning curve. It will take a few pages (no more, I hope) to adjust to the author's writing style. To the protagonist's voice. To obtain a firm understanding of who the main characters are and their relationships to one another. To understand where the story is going and to comprehend the goal, the problem to be solved.

And where and when this is all taking place.

Setting matters.

Of course, as a practical matter, the reader may already know the setting, having read the Amazon sales page or the summary on the back cover. But they want to see it again inside the book. They want to feel located in a certain place and time. Once they understand where they are, they can enjoy the story. Even if this location data is as vague as "A long time ago in a galaxy far, far away…" they've still been told what they need to know to settle in and enjoy the story.

I remember taking a pitch at a conference from an author who had written a charming tale set in an unspecified era of the rural American past. The story was rich with nostalgia and had a lovely *To Kill a Mockingbird* vibe—but I was troubled by the fact that the story never told me where or when it took place. Finally, I just asked. The response? "I didn't want to specify a place. I wanted the reader to see it as a universal archetype. Anytown USA. And I didn't want to fix it in a specific time period. It doesn't matter. It's not a history book. So I left that out."

Big mistake.

In the first place, you can achieve universality without leaving your story stranded in some non-existent neverland. The afore-mentioned *To Kill a Mockingbird* seems timeless, although we know it was set in a specific place—Maycomb, Alabama, filling in for Harper Lee's hometown, Monroeville, Alabama—during the Depression years in the sadly racist deep South. Do we know when and where the story happened? Of course. And yet it has enormous resonance today, not as a history book, but as a story confronting issues still very much with us, which is why the book continues to sell millions of copies a year.

When you give your reader the location, you're issuing an invitation. *Hey! I've created this marvelous world. Won't you join me? We're going to have an adventure!* Ideally, your story should be full of promise and intrigue, which is why you should avoid default choices like setting a book when and where you live because the protagonist is really a glamorized version of yourself…but we'll get back to that later.

Carefully considered description gives your reader access to the story—even when it's a place they've never been and know nothing about. Even if it's a time and place entirely of your own creation. You open the door, leave it ajar—and hope others will join you. If the invitation is enticing enough, it should work not only for the story but also for the book description on the online sales page—which is probably the most important piece of marketing you have these days. Frankly, I doubt that I would have wanted to visit racist Depression-era Monroeville, Georgia —but I've read *To Kill a Mockingbird* over and over again. Maycomb isn't just about bigotry—it's about a devoted single parent, a loving housekeeper, and neighbors who exemplify what a community should be. You might argue that the invitation exceeds the reality. But isn't that what the best books always do?

Skillful description has a transformative impact on your book.

Establishing the Right Tone

Description can be useful in setting tone, another important matter that needs to be established early in your story. Readers want to know what they're reading. Is this story funny? Tragic? Nostalgic? Formal? Casual? Description can help here. Another of Leonard's famous rules is: "Never open a book with weather." In fact, that's Rule Number One. I get where he's coming from. I too have seen many unpublished manuscripts opening with a description of the sunrise or a cold breeze. I don't worry about it much. The writer is just warming up. Once they get the story started it should be fine—and all this weather stuff can be cut. I think we can agree that describing the irrelevant climate is probably not the most effective way to draw readers into the story.

Unless it is…

Remember King Lear shouting "Blow, winds, and crack your cheeks!" Not the opening, but a good bit just the same. That Shakespeare guy had a knack for making the trivial significant. Remember the lengthy description of the tumultuous moors in the early pages of *Wuthering Heights*? The title keys you into it —"wuthering" is a provincial spin on "weathering," meaning nasty weather. (Heck, even Winnie-the-Pooh had a blustery day.)

These passages are not really about the weather. The authors are using weather to set the tone and to provide insight. Lear's soliloquy is about himself and the chaos he has created with one disastrously poor decision. Similarly, the windswept moors reflect the passions swirling in and around the people who live there, especially the brooding Heathcliff (Wuthering Heights is the name of his home) and the more excitable Cathy. Dickens opens his best novel, *Bleak House*, with "Fog everywhere. Fog up the river, where it flows among green aits and meadows; fog down the river, where it rolls defiled among the tiers of shipping, and the waterside pollutions of a great (and dirty) city." Why the weather report, Chuck? Because, as we're about to learn, the fog pervading London is mirrored by the fog throughout Chancery Court, the network of lawyers, judges, and laws that destroys lives.

Have you noticed how often sad scenes in movies are set in the rain? Creating rain on a movie set is technically difficult and expensive. No one would do it without a good reason. But you see it time and again, especially when characters are breaking up or experiencing other emotional turmoil. (Gene Kelly's memorable singing and dancing in a studio downpour is an outlier.) Karen Carpenter, in perhaps her moodiest hit, reminded us that "rainy days and Mondays always get me down." The weather is a reflection of the depression within.

Remember—you're not just creating these scenes for your own benefit. The reader has to come along for the ride. The reader has to feel the tone, the mood, the ambiance. Skillful description can help you put that across.

FINDING THE BED THAT'S JUST RIGHT

ALL OF THE SUGGESTIONS IN THIS BOOK COME WITH A PROVISO. IN the post-Einstein universe, everything is relative, and never more so than in writing, a field in which absolute rules do not exist. How much description you can get away with is relative, dependent upon the book you're writing. I find all these divisions and categorizations of books problematic and occasionally offensive, but I will use standard terms to explain what I mean. If you're writing literary fiction, pacing is less urgent and your readers may be able to tolerate more leisurely description—but even then, the reader's patience is not infinite. Beautiful words and phrases are often appreciated out of context, but in context, they tend to yank people out of the story, which diminishes reader immersion, which diminishes reader enjoyment. Popular fiction demands a fast pace, and never more so than in the present era, where entertainment is plentiful and a new book can be downloaded in seconds.

You must find your Goldilocks level of description, the amount that, for your story, is just right. You probably won't get there in the first draft. Here's the reality—writing is hard, and it isn't hard just for you. It's hard for everyone, because nothing in the world is more challenging than filling a blank screen with words. All writers edit, usually cutting more in subsequent drafts than they add. If a word, phrase, or sentence isn't advancing the story one way or another, it needs to go. And that is never more true than with description. So as you read the following chapters, bear in mind—it's not about how much description you write, and it's about how well you write it.

HIGHLIGHTS/EXERCISES

Highlights

1) You want readers to read your book, not skim it.

2) When readers see something that doesn't interest them, they skip it.

3) Reader engagement is key to reader enjoyment.

4) Don't let description undermine the pace.

5) Description matters.

6) Setting matters.

7) Skillful description has a transformative impact on your book.

Red Sneaker Exercises

1) Can you think of a memorable piece of descriptive prose

you've read recently? Something that stuck in your mind? (If not, maybe you've been skipping them, too.) Find that passage and read it again. What makes this stand out? Is it the lovely choice of words? The insight it gives to character? Does it advance the story, or is it just pretty words for the sake of pretty words? Once you've determined what you responded to, you can start contemplating how to create a similar effect in your own work.

2) Pick a scene in your work-in-progress that requires some description. Write two versions of the descriptive passage—the first, using as many words as you like, and the second, using as few words as possible. Which version do you prefer? Which works best for the story you're writing? Could you create a third version, a compromise draft that incorporates the best aspects of both?

3) Open the last book you read that you really liked. Look at the first page. How did the author establish the tone? How did you know what kind of narrative you were reading? Chances are, it was done right up front and economically, perhaps on the first page or even in the first sentence. Can you create a similar sentence for your book, one that establishes the tone and kick-starts the story, giving readers just as much description as they need?

2

LESS IS MORE

"Description begins in the writer's imagination, but should finish in the reader's."

— STEPHEN KING

Description causes plenty of problems for writers, both new and experienced. How much does the reader need to know? When do I quit? Do they need to know the hair color, eye color, and attire of every character who walks onto the stage? And then there is the matter of setting, which sometimes gets the opposite treatment. Early writers often spend too much time worrying about description—and too little developing setting.

Here's my overriding principle when it comes to description: **Less is more.**

Or to put it another way:

The best description is often the least description.

DOING MORE WITH LESS

. . .

DEPENDING UPON WHETHER YOU PREFER POETRY OR ARCHITECTURE, you may feel I'm stealing from Browning or Van Der Rohe—and you're right, either way. But this principle is equally applicable to writing, and never more so than when we're talking about description. If you apply this principle consistently, it answers many nagging questions. How much does the reader need to know? As little as possible to thoroughly understand the characters and their environment. How much is too much? One word more.

When I first started writing, I wanted to describe everything. Every time new characters entered, I stopped the story cold to provide a long-winded description of their coloring, attire, car of choice, drink of choice, body size, shoes, facial hair, etc. Borrrring. Most of those details didn't matter. They didn't illuminate the character or even help the reader form a better mental image—because most of that detail was lost. As soon as I said the character was a lawyer, or a doctor, or a corporate bigwig, readers had a mental image (based upon their own past experiences) and it wasn't going to be altered by my chatter about hair color, most of which was assigned arbitrarily. ("Let's see, the last female was blonde, so this one should be a brunette.") This trivia didn't stick with readers—because it had no inherent importance.

Don't bury the reader in unneeded description.

I remember the scene I wrote for *Primary Justice* when Ben Kincaid first entered a courtroom. I spent an entire page describing the courtroom in meticulous detail. During his line edit, my editor at Ballantine, Joe Blades, drew a red slash across the entire page. In the margin he wrote: "Everyone knows what a courtroom looks like." And he was right.

Don't waste your readers' time telling them what they already know—or don't need to know.

Perhaps you're thinking—wait a minute, buster, some of my

favorite books contain abundant description—and that's part of what I love about them. Think of the long languorous descriptions in many Victorian and post-Victorian novels. What Edith Wharton could do with a ballroom! Henry James could do a page-and-a-half on the shape of a women's face. Jane Austen could go on and on about the beauty of the countryside.

You need to realize that those writers wrote for a very different audience. During the nineteenth century, novel reading was the principal leisure-time activity of the leisure class. Books were often published as "triple-deckers," and if you were going to fill three volumes, you couldn't be too brief about anything. Photography either didn't exist or was restricted to the wealthy, and of course there was no television. Everyone hadn't already seen everything. There was good reason to describe the countryside for those who had never been exposed to it, or foreign dress, or fancy balls, or even a courtroom. Those writers weren't duplicating what readers had already conjured in their minds' eyes. They were supplying essential information.

More often than not, whatever you choose to describe, even if your book is set in the future or a galaxy far, far away, your readers have already seen it. As a result, to steal a term from the art world, modern-day writers are mostly minimalists. They suggest rather than exhaust. They point readers in the proper direction, then trust them to carry the description the rest of the way home.

READERS ARE YOUR PARTNERS

I'VE ALWAYS LOVED LISTENING TO RECORDINGS OF OLD-TIME RADIO, shows like *The Shadow* and *Inner Sanctum* from the Golden Age of radio drama. (If you haven't had the pleasure, they're readily available on the internet, and today, some podcasts are trying to create the same sort of aural drama.) These broadcasts had no visual elements at all—and yet, it's amazing how little description the shows provided—or needed. Typically, a narrator, often a first-person narrator, would set the time and place, and after that, all descriptive information would be supplied by the dialogue and sound effects. Sometimes that was a bit awkward —"Don't point that gun you just drew out of your holster at me!" But overall, these hot-blooded dramas demonstrate how well a story can be told without overt description. They left room for the audience to exercise their imaginations.

Often, when a movie is based upon a well-read book, fans go into an uproar over the casting, filling cyberspace with nasty tweets and bulletin board posts. Remember when Tom Cruise was cast to play Lestat in *Interview with a Vampire?* The outrage! He looks nothing like Lestat! Well, actually, if you go back and read the description in the book, Cruise in the film looks a great deal like Lestat in the book (except shorter). Even the book's author, Anne Rice, initially an opponent of the casting, later admitted he embodied the character well. So why the outrage?

All the details on the printed page didn't matter nearly so much as the image readers conjured in their mind's eye when they read the book. They knew what (they thought) Lestat looked like. And apparently no one had imagined Tom Cruise. The same phenomenon occurs almost every time a literary character is embodied on the screen. Readers have to adjust their mental images to those provided by Hollywood, remembering that this is an adaptation, not a duplication—so be flexible. (But don't get me started on Tom Cruise as Jack Reacher. That was just wrong.)

Trust your reader. Let the reader fill in the blanks.

THE BEST DESCRIPTIONS PROVIDE SUBTLE INSIGHT

. . .

IF DETAILED DESCRIPTION ISN'T IMPORTANT, WHAT IS? IN MY book *Creating Character*, I wrote about the difference between character and characterization, and suggested selecting one or two salient details that: 1) readers will remember, and 2) give readers insight into who this character is. These telling details are probably not going to be eye color or height or other accidents of birth. But a person's car does give the reader insight into that person, and might help create a vivid mental image. The clothes they wear. The meals they order. Jewelry, purse, shoes. Don't assign these details randomly. Think about the essence of the character, and how you're going to show that to the reader without explicitly stating it.

These details can be provided without stopping the story. Economy in description produces better results than mounds of detail, intellectual overload, words poured on words. A novel at its core is storytelling, and if the story bogs down and doesn't engage the reader, it is unlikely to succeed. No words are elegant enough if the reader is bored. Sentences burdened with adjectives and adverbs are slower to read and harder to process. Adjectives suggest that you need a more specific noun and adverbs suggest that you need a more precise verb. Forget those crutches and instead find *le mot juste*—the perfect word or phrase to economically convey what you want to say.

The best approach is not abundant description—but abundant observation. It's not about how much, it's about how well. Learn to pay attention. Watch the people around you. Seek out the details that others might not notice—but that provide insight into the situation or the characters in it. Observe the world and collect the telling details—the couple on the next row in the subway train, the family at the restaurant table behind you, the homeless guy at the bus station. The single man carefully folding a handkerchief. The elderly woman on the park bench eating plums.

Focus on sparing description that provides insight.

Writers are the pack rats of the universe, watching, observing, collecting, recording. Writers should always be harvesting experiences and storing them away till they can be used. I can recall instances when I brought back a conversation I'd heard ten years before—because it was exactly what I needed for a particular scene, to give it the authenticity or insight it required. I recommend that you carry a journal with you at all times so nothing is lost or forgotten. (If you want to dictate into your phone, fine, but many studies have shown that ideas have more impact and are retained longer when you physically write them down.) Edward Hopper carried a journal, and one day he noticed an entry about some people he spotted at an all-night diner. You probably know how that turned out.

What observation will trigger your masterpiece?

One last thought.

The best observations are linked to emotion.

The old woman on the park bench could evoke pathos—or joy—depending upon how the description is written. The single man with the handkerchief could suggest loneliness—or an orderly mind. What emotions you evoke depend upon how well, how accurately—and perhaps how economically—you describe it.

HIGHLIGHTS/EXERCISES

Highlights

1) Less is more.

2) The best description is often the least description.

3) Don't bury the reader in unneeded character description.

4) Don't waste your reader's time telling them what they already know—or don't need to know.

5) Trust your reader. Let the reader fill in the blanks.

6) Focus on sparing description that provides insight.

7) The best observations are linked to emotion.

Red Sneaker Exercises

1) Do you carry a journal with you? If not, you should. You

almost certainly carry a cellphone, so if you have an aversion to carrying a Moleskine (as Hemingway did), open the Notes app. You can even dictate your notes, if typing on tiny devices is not your strong suit. Next time you see or overhear something interesting or unusual, make a note. (You could even take a picture or video, assuming no one objects). Store those notes somewhere safe. Review them from time to time. When you're ready to use the experience in your writing, you'll have something to jog your memory.

2) Pull out your work-in-progress and find an important descriptive passage. Could you do more with less? Can you reduce a paragraph to a sentence? Can you extract the one character detail that gives the reader insight into who this person is? Be careful not to resort to clichés. Devise your own metaphors.

3) Take the challenge in the last paragraph of this chapter. Write a descriptive passage involving an elderly woman on a park bench, or a couple at a late-night diner. Can you give the description emotional content? Can you use your descriptive words to create an emotional feeling—without overt heartstring-tugging or sentimentality?

4) What level of description is appropriate for the kind of book you're writing? Robert E. Howard's sword-and-sorcery stories are renowned for their pulpy hot-blooded descriptions—but that wouldn't work in a serious kitchen-sink drama or a coming-of-age novel. What works in the coming-of-age drama might seem tedious in a fast-paced fantasy. What level of description will work best in the book you're writing?

3

SENSORY DESCRIPTION

"All we have to believe is our senses: the tools we use to perceive the world, our sight, our touch, our memory."

— NEIL GAIMAN

One year I discussed description at WriterCon in the midst of a talk titled "Five Super-Secret Steps to Superior Fiction." Obviously, I chose this title primarily due to my addiction to alliteration, but also because the elements of great session topics are, first, numbered lists, and second, the suggestion that you're revealing secrets. The problem, of course, was that having devised this brilliant title, I needed to come up with an equally brilliant list of super-secrets.

I don't know how brilliant the talk was, but I did generate a list. And one of the super-secret steps related to description. I didn't notice the audience looking as if I'd revealed the arcane secrets of the ancients when I said, Less is more. But I finally saw eyes widen when I said:

You have five senses. Use them all.

What did that mean?

TRIANGULATE THE READER

INSTEAD OF RELENTLESSLY (AND MONOTONOUSLY) DESCRIBING HOW your fictional environment appears, you should also evoke how the character's surroundings smell or feel. You should write about what the character hears and perhaps even tastes. You should use all five senses to create a more powerful portrait. **Use all five senses in your descriptions.**

Does this mean your description must be lengthier? Not necessarily. In the first place, you don't have to use all five senses every time you describe. You use what seems relevant, evocative, appropriate for the scene you're writing. Furthermore, if you eliminate every unneeded word, you will find you can do a great deal with a minimum of verbiage.

In one of his short stories, "Lost in the Funhouse," John Barth described his approach to description. Mind you, this is a work of fiction, but employing the meta-fictional techniques Barth loved so well, the story becomes a treatise on writing technique. Barth doesn't entirely eschew visual description, but he suggests combining it with description employing one or more of the other senses. "The procedure may be compared to the way surveyors and navigators determine their position by two or more compass bearings, a process of triangulation." **Use sight plus one or more of the other senses to triangulate the reader.**

I have noticed that when early writers start describing, they typically describe how something looks. In other words, they use only one sense—sight. This is understandable. Sight is the sense we exercise most often. When people think about description, they typically imagine how something looks. I've even attended workshops where speakers told readers to "Imagine your scene on a television screen. Write what you see."

This is horrible advice. Limiting yourself to one sense is like typing with one finger. Why? Describing only appearances too often leads to the most superficial and least impactful descriptions. You're basically telling readers what they conjured in their minds' eyes the instant you said "courtroom" or "blanket" or "sunset." And if they already have a mental image of the scene, no description from you is likely to dislodge it.

Each of the other senses can make unique contributions:

Sound: Dialogue would be the most obvious example of bringing your viewpoint character's sense of hearing into play, but there are many other ways to use this that aren't dependent upon the sound's content. Loud crashing noises can create tension or unease. Piercing sounds, like sirens, can create a sense of danger. Whispering can create intimacy. Mentioning a familiar song can be enormously evocative. As soon as you mention the title, the reader may begin hearing the melody. It might not always be appropriate for a character to taste her surroundings, but almost every environment has a sound, so this is usually available to help you create the needed ambiance.

Try to avoid too much onomatopoeia. Readers tire fast of "jangle" and "crash" and similar sound-effect words.

Smell: Vladimir Nabokov wrote, "Nothing revives the past so completely as a smell that was once associated with it." Scientists say that smell is the sense most closely linked to memory. As a result, smelling something associated with a previous time or place can be a powerful way of evoking it. If you're trying to create a sense of nostalgia, or if you're writing a flashback, the sense of smell might kick the reader's olfactory memory into high gear. For that matter, describing an unpleasant odor can create an apprehensive or unpleasant feeling. Think about the power of words like "reeked" or "stank" or "pungent."

Touch: Due to the inherently tactile nature of the sense of touch, it is often associated with various forms of intimacy. You don't normally touch something—or someone—unless you are comfortable with them. When you do touch something, you immediately note the texture and the temperature. The texture suggests a certain reaction or mood. Soft fabrics are comforting. Harsh or abrasive surfaces are unsettling and chill-inducing.

The temperature also creates a mood. Warm surfaces are appealing, but cold surfaces are off-putting. Thrillers often involve fights, torture, or other forms of physical contact that may be linked to pain, the dark but powerful negative aspect of touch.

Taste: This may be the most difficult of the senses to effectively convey in a book, but it can be done, and can be incredibly powerful when done right. Obviously, it only arises when characters are using their lips and tongues, which generally means eating, drinking, or loving. A little goes a long way, since you're describing sensations the reader has experienced and will immediately recall. Having a character enjoy the creamy delights of ice cream will surely induce happiness. Having a character taste something foul or bitter should have the opposite effect. You probably don't need to go on at length about how bacon tastes or why people love it. Your reader already knows. Remember that in many ways, taste is a synthesis of many senses. Texture and smell and sometimes even sight combine to create taste.

Use the sensory description that best fits the scene you're writing.

As always, what works best will depend upon your scene. But if it's early morning for your character, it's hard to imagine anything better than a bracing cup of coffee—and coffee involves a rich aroma, a warm temperature, and a bitter taste. William Carlos Williams memorably wrote a poem about a "poor old woman" sitting on a park bench eating plums—which are cool on the lips and sweet on the tongue. "They taste good to her."

. . .

Description Sets the Tone

Early writers tend toward pleasant, appealing descriptions —lots of sunsets and wind-whipped ocean currents—even when the book is a mystery or thriller. Regardless of your genre, you want your story to have tension, to give readers the feeling that all is not as it should be. That's how you keep readers turning pages. You can't do that with rambling portraits of idyllic landscapes. You use skillful description to bring a scene to life, and to inject tension—by using all of your senses in close collaboration.

Use skillful description to create tension.

Let me take you through an example.

He laid on the comforter.

Not a terribly exciting sentence, is it? Let's dress it up with some description.

He laid on the black comforter.

Oh, good work, Bill. Much better. You added an adjective. You took something that should be, well, comforting—a comforter—and turned it into something dull and uninteresting —black. Surely we can do better without interrupting the pace of this obviously breathtaking story.

He laid on the comforter. It stank of sweat.

.   .   .

A LITTLE BETTER. ONE STRONG WORD IS BETTER THAN A DOZEN weak ones, and "stank" is a strong word that immediately conjures a powerful sensory image. You can almost smell the stink. Plus, the comforter is sweaty, which means it feels wet and icky. So now we've activated three senses—sight, touch, smell. I'm not going to make the guy taste the sweaty comforter, but we could still improve this…

HE LAID ON A BLACK SCRATCHY COMFORTER THAT STANK OF SWEAT.

YOU CAN DECIDE FOR YOURSELF WHETHER YOU PREFER TWO SHORT sentences or one slightly longer one. To some extent, the choice depends upon the pace you're creating. If this is a tense, suspenseful, scary scene, go with the short sentences. Longer sentences create a more leisurely pace.

The primary addition in the last example is the word "scratchy." This adds another unpleasant suggestion about how the comforter feels—and perhaps a sound cue as well. Scratchy things make noise, so the overall takeaway is irritating, perhaps grating. To create tension, you've decribed a comforter, something we normally think of as pleasant, and instead made it just the opposite, by employing a few, brief, descriptive words. It's black. Blah. Stinks. Ick. Sweaty. Gross. And scratchy. Something you want to get rid of, not wrap around yourself. You've only used a few words, but you've created a vivid, emotional picture that will have far more impact on the reader than a long-winded description based solely upon sight.

Tension is just one example of a mood that can be established through skillful description. A good approach to every scene is to remind yourself what emotional tone you're striving for before you write it. Is this scene romantic? Suspenseful? Humorous?

Heart-breaking? When you have a clear idea what you want, you're far more likely to achieve it. What emotions you evoke will depend upon how well you describe the scene. Remember that you have five senses and use them all.

HIGHLIGHTS/EXERCISES

Highlights

1) Use all five senses in your descriptions.

2) Use sight plus one or more of the other senses to triangulate the reader.

3) Use the sensory description that best fits the scene you're writing.

4) Use skillful description to create tension.

Red Sneaker Exercises

1) Leave your writer's garret and go someplace interesting, someplace filled with people and action. Find a comfortable place to sit, open your journal...and pay attention. You will likely first notice what you see, but what else can you detect? What do you smell? What do you hear? If there are sensations of touch and

taste, consider those as well. How can you best convey these sensations to the reader?

2) When you're writing a scene in a new location, think about where you could go to absorb the ambiance you'll be describing. It doesn't have to be the exact place in your book, just someplace similar. One beach, or office building, or courtroom, may work as well as another. Make a record of the sensory observations you collected during your visit. Then incorporate them into your work, not adding description just for the sake of description, but where it can help bring the location or characters to life.

3) Ever have the experience of hearing a song on the radio and immediately recalling an important time in your life that you associate with that song? Or is it a pleasant aroma that takes you back in time? You can provide that same sensory connection to your readers by evoking smell, sounds, songs, movies, clothing styles, and other relics from the past.

4) In your outline, add the relevant sensory impressions for each scene. This may be best saved until after you have the plot in place and you're looking to enhance the outline to improve the quality of your first draft. Look at the setting of the scene. Is it interesting enough? Could you make it better? People don't always have to meet in the obvious place. What would be more interesting? Once you have the location, make a list of sensory impressions—what is your character likely to see, hear, touch, smell, taste at that location? Even if you only have one entry in each category, it will likely add spice to the scene.

5) If you're writing popular fiction, you may focus on plot more than you do description. Go through your work-in-progress and look for places where a little description might be welcome, might prevent each scene from looking like all the others.

Remember, the added description does not have to be lengthy. How can you use as few words as possible but still inject a sense of location—plus a few sensory details to bring that location to life?

6) Writers have a tendency to rely too much on cliché, especially in first drafts, when the words are flying and you're not focused as much on language as in later drafts. You may have description that isn't really describing, like "The room smelled like death" or "She looked like she'd been rode hard and put away wet." These are metaphors, not true description, and rely more on familiarity than insight. Look through your manuscripts and see if you can replace these phrases with more powerful sensory description.

4

STEALTH DESCRIPTION

"Warmth. Wind. Dancing blue waters, and the sound of the waves. I see, hear, feel them all still."

— MARGARET GEORGE

After reading about how some readers dislike description and tend to skip it, you may be wondering whether you want any description in your book at all. The answer, of course, is that you do, but you probably won't get the balance exactly right in the first draft. You will never get a precise definition from me or anyone else of how much description is enough. I would love to announce The Bernhardt Rule: Five Descriptive Words Per Paragraph—but that would be nonsense. This is a decision you will always have to make in context, taking into account the pace of the story and the reader's need to know.

What should you do when you realize a story needs a little description, or the reader needs to know something about the surroundings, but you can't afford to slow the story down? I have two suggestions: stealth description, and its close companion, figurative language. Both approaches have a common denominator. They are both ways of writing description that doesn't look like description.

Use stealth description to provide essential information.

Making Description Invisible

The central idea behind what I call stealth description is that you give the reader enough to visualize the scene without writing anything that strikes the reader as descriptive. Hence the stealth part. It's like mashing your children's vegetables and mixing them into the ice cream. (Please don't do that.) The reader gets what's good for them, without feeling that they been forced to read something that didn't interest them.

Take a look at this passage of less-than-scintillating prose:

Jack walked into the principal's office. It had a chair behind a big desk. There was a file folder on the desk with Jack's name on the cover. A drawer in a file cabinet was open. He sat in a chair and waited nervously.

Are you spellbound? Probably not. The action and the description are completely distinct. First the action—the viewpoint character enters the principal's office, a move that likely fills him with dread, though we get little sense of that until the end. The next two sentences are by-the-book description that adds nothing to the mental image you conjured in your mind the instant you read the words "principal's office." If the description isn't adding anything readers can't imagine on their own—why bother? At the end of the paragraph, the passage reverts to action, continuing the thread initiated by the first sentence.

The description is entirely sight-based. No other senses are invoked. You have serious style offenses—like sentences beginning with indefinite pronouns, "It had" and "There was." The last sentence is all that gives you any indication of the character's emotional state, but that is accomplished in the clunkiest, most "telling" way possible—with an adverb. Not by describing his nervous body language, or the physiological impact of the environment. Not even by choosing an evocative verb, like "trembled." Through an adverb.

Bleh.

Take a look at this paragraph:

Jack dragged himself into the principal's office, sank into a chair opposite the desk, and stared at the wooden paddle swinging from a nail.

Now we have some actual stealth description, although I still think this could be better (and you will be invited to make it so in the Exercises). Now there is not a single sentence that exists just for the sake of description. All the descriptive elements have been integrated with the action, and perhaps even more importantly, integrated with verbs that are not stillborn but rife with emotion. Now Jack "dragged" himself into the office and "sank" beside the desk. The reader gets the description, but the most powerful takeaway is the emotional content of the sentence, as it should be.

Similarly, instead of the pointless file folder, we now have a paddle presenting a lurking threat. (If you find the concept of corporal punishment too disturbing, have Jack obsess on a truant officer.) You're told that the viewpoint character stares at the paddle, but you're not told why. Because you already know why. He's scared. The passage doesn't tell the reader Jack was scared, and didn't resort to any clunky adverbs. The reader has more than enough to visualize the scene, to feel the tension, and you accomplished that without slowing the pace and without writing a single word the average reader would recognize as description. With enormous economy, without a wasted word, you've not only established the setting but dramatized your character's reaction to the setting.

Stealth description integrates description with action and emotion.

FIGURATIVE LANGUAGE

WHEN I USE THE TERM "FIGURATIVE LANGUAGE," I'M REFERRING TO all those rhetorical devices you probably learned—and possibly learned to despise—in high school English. I'm talking about simile, metaphor, personification, analogy, and all their related brethren. Used sparingly and precisely, they can be effective tools for providing description without appearing to describe— another form of stealth description. Used too frequently, of course, they can become showy and annoying. Used imprecisely, they can produce head-scratching rather than insight. As always, you will search for the "Goldilocks" level—the amount and type of figurative language that is "just right" for your story.

Figurative language can provide descriptive information in a way that surprises and delights.

I'll discuss four of the many types of figurative language: similes, metaphors, personification, and allusions.

Similes can describe without appearing to describe.

As I'm sure you recall, similes compare one thing to another, typically using "like" or "as." The result may be poetic, but the real benefit is that although the simile describes, it looks nothing like traditional description.

. . .

THE CITY SKYLINE WAS TO ME LIKE A HOT FUDGE SUNDAE WAS TO my father.

SEE WHAT HAPPENED THERE? YOU'VE JUST DESCRIBED THE CITY FOR the reader without appearing to describe it. You told the reader that the viewpoint character thinks it's beautiful (or perhaps scrumptious) without going into a lot of detail about shimmering skyscrapers or dazzling neon signs. Moreover, you've given the reader your character's emotional reaction to the city.

Here's another example from possibly the greatest novelist who ever lived, Charles Dickens, describing someone who is depressed and devastated:

HE LOOKED LIKE HIS OWN SHADOW AT SUNSET.

OF COURSE, CHUCK COULD HAVE SIMPLY SAID THE CHARACTER WAS depressed, but he was much too talented a writer for that. Instead, he painted an image, both visual and emotional, through the skillful use of a well-wrought simile. This is a concise description that never tempts the reader to employ speed-reading skills. The pace of the story has not been slowed, but the image is far more powerful than one that might have taken a page. When you write a story, you're encouraging the reader to suspend belief, to enter this magical dream you've created. Anything that looks like an overt description may wake them from the dream.

In *Primary Justice*, I wrote:

. . .

DEREK SUCKED ON THE CIGARETTE AS IF HE WERE DRAWING THE smoke in from another galaxy.

OK, SO I'M NOT AS SUBTLE AS DICKENS. BUT I THINK YOU GET THE idea. This worked well for this novel, since it conveyed its image with a small dose of humor, something I used throughout that book to alleviate the protagonist's tension and the dire plotline. I described what happened and also provided some insight into the character—but I doubt many readers felt they had been subjected to description.

Metaphors imply descriptive information.

Metaphors do much the same thing, but the comparison is implied rather than overt. You ditch the "like" or "as." Often the joy of the metaphor is the surprise—you indicate that two things which at first seem nothing alike are in fact similar in some meaningful way that gives readers the insight you want them to have. When Shakespeare wrote that, "All the world's a stage, and all the men and women merely players..." he didn't mean the description to be taken literally. He used a metaphor to comment on the artificiality of daily life, the sense of a grand scheme over which we have little control.

So you might be inclined to say:

SHAKESPEARE, THAT REMARKABLE BRITISH LION, POSSESSED uncommon perception about the complexities of everyday life.

I THINK I CAN SAFELY ASSUME YOU ARE ALREADY AWARE THAT Shakespeare was not in fact a lion. The metaphor was meant to suggest that he was the king of his jungle, an unparalleled poet whose words were so profound that they stand above all the others. Of course, I could have simply said, "That Bill Shakespeare could really write," but it would not have the same impact. The example sentence describes him and his work in a way that is more interesting and does not feel like description.

Personification can be used to describe indirectly what might be boring or obvious if described directly.

Personification is a specific form of metaphor that describes something that is not human doing something humans do, as in "The sun smiled down upon us." Yes, we know the sun is actually a big ball of gas not capable of smiling, but a sentence like this describes the temperature without seeming like a bland weather report.

Allusion can provide descriptive information by referencing other works.

An allusion is simply one work of art borrowing from another. In the modern-day metafictional universe, this has become far too common, and as a result, I would avoid it, at least unless it truly provides stealth description you can't get any other way. The world is too full of references to *Star Wars*, *The Wizard of Oz*, *Gone With the Wind*, and *The Godfather*. (The exception of course is *Star Trek*, which never grows old.) The other problem is that references to trendy television programs, actors, movies, memes, videos, or even books, may date your work, and you don't want that in this world of electronic and print-on-demand books that need never go out of print.

There may still be some occasions when a clever or insightful reference to another work may add an additional dimension to your work. Robert Frost's poem "Out, Out" obviously references the famous "Out, out, brief candle" speech from *Macbeth*. Frost essentially incorporates by reference the theme of the original, the uncertainty and brevity of life, without having to actually say or describe any of that.

A popular young adult novel by John Green is titled *The Fault in Our Stars*, an allusion to *Julius Caesar*, another play by Shakespeare. (That guy really gets around.) Here, Green inverts the meaning of the original quotation to describe his central theme—the unfairness of the universe. In the original play, Brutus says, "The fault, dear Brutus, is not in our stars, but in ourselves..." But in Green's book, his lead characters, Hazel and Gus, who both suffer from forms of juvenile cancer, are clearly not to blame for their tragic fate.

One of my favorite novels, Kurt Vonnegut's *Cat's Cradle*, begins "Call me Jonah. My parents did, or nearly did." This is obviously a reference to the famous opening line of Moby-Dick: "Call me Ishmael." Vonnegut references the classic novel in part to make a joke—the viewpoint character's name is actually John, about as bland and unliterary as it gets. But the reference also suggests that John is also about to embark on a mythic journey, though one very different from that described by Melville.

Many other types of figurative language exist—analogies, symbolism, elevated language, minimalist language, and on and on. But you get the idea. Making a comparison is another way of describing something without appearing to describe it, another way of providing information to your reader without slowing the pace of your story.

HIGHLIGHTS/EXERCISES

Highlights

1) Use stealth description to provide essential information.

2) Stealth description integrates description with action and emotion.

3) Figurative language can provide descriptive information in a way that surprises and delights.

4) Similes can be used to describe without describing.

5) Metaphors imply descriptive information.

6) Personification can be used to describe indirectly what might be boring or obvious if described directly.

7) Allusion can provide descriptive information by incorporating other works.

Red Sneaker Exercises

1) Earlier in this chapter, I provided a brief description of a boy named Jack who entered the principal's office. Can you improve this example of stealth description? Give the scene more depth. Elaborate. Don't make it longer just for the sake of being longer, but look for ways to increase the tension, to provide more insight into Jack and his situation.

2) Find a descriptive passage in your work-in-progress. Is there a way to provide the same degree of description, whatever is truly needed, without appearing to describe? Can you build it into the action? Can you replace boring verbs with words that have more emotional content?

3) Think about the lead character in your work-in-progress. Write a sentence describing that character using each of the four examples of figurative language discussed in this chapter: simile, metaphor, personification, and allusion. Don't be redundant. Use each of the four sentences to describe another aspect of the character.

4) Find a particularly descriptive passage in your work-in-progress. Circle every adjective and adverb. Do you need them? Are they providing essential descriptive information? Consider ways of eliminating them. The usual way to eliminate an adverb is to supply a more precise or descriptive verb. The usual way to replace an adjective is to improve the noun it describes, although you may find many instances when you can simply cut it with no loss to the tale.

5

DESCRIBING CHARACTERS

"In displaying the psychology of your characters, minute particulars are essential. God save us from vague generalizations!"

— ANTON CHEKHOV

Describing the characters in your story can be challenging. The reader has to know what the characters look like. And they won't know unless you tell them, right? As is so often the case in the world of writing, the answer is yes and no. Your readers should have a mental image of the characters, but a good deal of that they can and will supply themselves, given the slightest prodding from the writer. And yes, they won't know what characters are like unless you tell them, but you don't need a litany of visual information to bring a character to life. To the contrary, it may be more important to indicate *who* the characters are than what they look like.

Describing a character should involve more than physical appearance.

. . .

DESCRIBING CHARACTERS TO LIFE (NOT TO DEATH)

MANY IF NOT MOST FIRST-TIME WRITERS FEEL A COMPULSION TO describe characters in minute detail the first time they appear in a book. No, it's not just you—I've been there too. But it's a mistake. Truth is, most of that kind of description has little impact on the reader. The moment you indicate who the character is, what they do, what role they play in the drama, the reader begins visualizing them. If you say the character is a doctor, they will conjure an image based upon doctors they have known or seen on television. If you say the character is a pirate, swashbuckling images will come to mind. The same is true for men, women, dogs, cats, barbarians, spaceship pilots, and everyone else.

This does not mean you can do nothing to alter these instantaneous associations. The question is whether you want to. If the character is not of great import, basically a "spear-carrier" who performs a specific plot function and then disappears, you may be content to let the reader have their way. With a more important character, you have a more specific image you want to establish. My suggestion is that you not be excessively detailed in either case. It will be easier to persuade a reader to remember a single salient item—a scarred cheek, an eccentric hairstyle, a bad habit—than a full-length Henry James body portrait.

The trick is to pick the right detail. You want something that will first, cause the reader to remember who that character is, and second, convey some important information about the character. In John Kennedy Toole's marvelous novel, *A Confederacy of Dunces*, we are told that our plus-size protagonist, Ignatius J. Reilly, wears a green hunters' cap with flaps over the ears. Toole got it in one—that was all I needed to fully envision this character.

In a typical novel, you will have somewhere between fifty and a hundred characters— but perhaps five who are most important. You want the reader to remember who those five are every time they appear. A telling descriptive element can serve as a mnemonic device. "Oh right, he's the guy who wants to take over the world." Even better if that memorable trait gives insight not just to identity but also to personality. "Oh right, he's the guy who was scarred fighting for a woman and now he's bitter and cynical about romance."

The best character descriptions have both an identifying and a defining aspect.

When I wrote *Primary Justice*, I worried about the reader remembering who all the characters were. Truth told, I worried about a lot of things, because I didn't know what I was doing. But I kept plugging away at it. I was particularly concerned about the reader remembering who a particular character was when he was finally revealed to be the murderer.

SPOILER ALERT! I am about to reveal too much about the plot of *Primary Justice*.

At its core, this novel is a mystery, so of course, the revelation of who committed the murder should be a surprise. Typically, the killer is the least likely suspect, which means they can't be too prominent or dominant throughout the book. I worried that when the veil dropped and the truth was uncovered—no one would remember who that guy was.

That's when I came up with his identifying trait. He tells lawyer jokes.

When I wrote the book, lawyer jokes were all the rage, despite relying upon negative stereotypes that today (I hope) would be considered cliché and hatemongering. But did this recurring tag provide insight into the character's personality? Big time. And it informed his relationship with the lead character, Ben Kincaid, a lawyer, who found the jokes seriously unfunny. Did it help the reader remember who the character was? Of course. He was the guy who told lawyer jokes every time he appeared. (Once I devised this tag, of course, I had to go back through the manuscript and add these bad jokes to all his scenes.)

It worked. The ending, with its layers of twists and reveals, satisfied readers. (And in case you're wondering, you can still read the novel, because I haven't revealed quite everything...)

The lesson? When you bring your new characters onstage for the first time, forget about burying readers with details they won't remember anyway. Instead, pick one or two traits that are worth hammering home—and leave the rest to the reader's imagination. Physical description is typically what sticks with readers least because it seems unimportant and, in many cases, random. Instead, portray the details that make a difference. And even those ideas don't have to drop the instant the character first appears. They can be sprinkled throughout the scene. Perhaps some could even be saved for the character's second appearance.

Unless a character's clothes, shoes, hairstyle, jewelry, etc., tell the reader something about the character, leave it out. The character will seem more vivid as a result, not less so. This is what I believe John Barth was implying in another passage from that short story, "Lost in the Funhouse." At one point, the narrator writes, "The brown hair on Ambrose's mother's forearms gleamed in the sun like."

No, that's not a typo. That's how the sentence ends. Like *what*?

And that's Barth's point. What difference does it make? In this case, none whatsoever, so he leaves it out. He lets his readers supply the detail—since they are likely to do so anyway. Let them have the pleasure of performing their function in this partnership, while you do your job with confidence and style.

Let the reader supply details that don't matter.

CHARACTER DESCRIPTION THAT MATTERS

. . .

THE DESCRIPTION THAT IS MOST DRAMATICALLY IMPORTANT HAS nothing to do with what kind of car your character drives or whether they wear matching socks. The description that will add tension, drama, and power to your narrative is the description of how your character impacts the other characters in the story.

Describe the impact your character has on others.

This is almost another form of both stealth description and sensory description because, once again, you're not strictly relying upon visuals, and you're supplying description that doesn't look like it. When you portray the impact one character has on another, you're deepening the drama, increasing the conflict, adding tension, adding complexity to your narrative.

The possibilities are endless. Does your character radiate animal magnetism or sexuality? This trait appears a great deal in romance novels, and you can readily understand why. One character's masculinity is likely to impact the other lead character, leading to a fiery romantic encounter.

Does a character's posture suggest weakness or insecurity? How do others react? Do they take advantage of him? Or, like Clark Kent, does the weakling act disarm people, or mask the power hidden within?

What you imply but don't say can have more impact than what you say.

If readers can draw conclusions from your descriptive details that you don't spell out, the reader will not only get the point but will feel smart—a veritable guarantee that they will like and appreciate your book.

One of my favorite examples is in Ian Fleming's novel *Goldfinger*. As you may recall, when James Bond and Auric Goldfinger first meet face to face, both knowing who the other is but pretending not to, they play golf. Goldfinger cheats, of course, being the bad guy—but surprise!—Bond cheats even worse. The telling detail comes when Goldfinger gets out his clubs. He's obviously spent a lot of money on them and yet, his clubs are each in individual plastic tubes. Fleming doesn't spell it out, but for anyone who plays golf, this is a sure sign that Goldfinger is a poseur.

Similarly, in *Rabbit is Rich*, the third of John Updike's Rabbit Angstrom books, the newly wealthy Rabbit is in Vegas playing blackjack, using a betting strategy he believes is foolproof. Every time he loses, he doubles his bet, so eventually he will recoup any loses. Except as anyone who knows anything about gambling realizes, this is a popular strategy—for suckers. Updike doesn't explain it in detail, but eventually, when a player loses four or five hands in a row (as Rabbit does), the doubling strategy will require a bet that exceeds his comfort level. The house wins, as always.

I'm not the first to note that one of the most beloved novels of the twentieth century, *To Kill a Mockingbird*, is about young Scout's discovery that her father, Atticus Finch, is a great man. And yet, at no point in the novel does Scout, or anyone else, expressly say that. We learn it by observing Atticus' actions— through her eyes—and the reactions she and others have to his actions. In the recent Broadway stage adaptation by Aaron Sorkin, this character portrait is made even more powerful by showing that, when the play opens, Atticus is a commonplace lawyer dealing with deeds and wills and not sticking his neck out for anyone. When a judge asks him to take the controversial defense of Jim, the black man accused of a horrible crime, Atticus rises to the challenge. Both Scout and—through her eyes—the audience see his character evolve, that is, see Atticus *become* a great man.

I hope you will forgive me for, once again, returning to *Primary Justice*, but there's a good example of this involving one of the lead characters, one of the most popular characters in the series. Why does Christina always wear those wacky outfits? Initially, I used this to distinguish her from the other characters. But as I continued writing, this evolved into an opportunity to provide insight into her character. This novel is set primarily inside a big corporate law firm, so everyone else is wearing essentially identical dress suits. But not Christina. She's wearing short skirts and colored leggings and anything else that suits her fancy. And she gets away with it. Why? Because she is very good at her job, so good the management tolerates her eccentricities.

This simple detail became the key to understanding who Christina truly is. It also indicated an effervescent non-conformist personality that made her so popular with readers.

Here's one more tidbit from *Primary Justice*. Throughout that book, and for that matter, throughout the eighteen Ben Kincaid novels that followed, I never provided any significant description of what the lead character looks like. Over time, you may get the impression that Ben is on the small side, thin, not tall. In a later book, someone mentions that Ben's getting a bald spot. But eye color? Hair color? Face shape? Never mentioned. What was portrayed was his never-give-up spirit, his intelligence, his kindness, his vulnerability, and his genuine concern for his clients and others. Despite the lack of descriptive detail, readers came to feel they knew Ben so well the series went to the bestseller lists— and I still get a steady stream of mail hoping Ben will appear again.

Physical description is not as important as descriptive details that bring the character to life.

Don't Base Characters on Real People

THIS SEEMS AS GOOD A POINT AS ANY TO CAUTION YOU AGAINST basing your characters on real people. This is dangerous, potentially ruinous, and frankly, not good writing. And yet everyone is tempted to do it, particularly when they start out as writers. Early writers' first protagonists tend to be glamorized versions of themselves, so it's not surprising that the protagonist's associates should be based upon persons the writer knows—the best friend, the co-worker, the next-door neighbor. The villain, of course, is the ex. Or perhaps the boss. Or a parent. And the book stops being about entertainment and starts being about vengeance.

This is a no-win scenario. You are playing with fire. In the first place, the object of your vengeance probably won't be troubled all that much by your scathing portrait. In fact, they may be flattered. But more to the point, they might sue, which will truly suck the fun out of your publishing experience. As I mentioned in *Creating Character*, you can weaken the case by adding unflattering details no one would want to suggest are true about themselves. But the better approach is to simply not go there in the first place.

Don't base your characters on real people you know or famous people you don't know.

Does this real person you know have one distinctive characteristic that could be useful in the story? Fine, take that one characteristic and change everything else. At some point, you will realize that you don't need to crib from your circle of associates to write a good book. Often, this is simply a shortcut—but not one that will likely improve your story.

If you think there is any chance someone might believe one of your fictional characters is based upon someone you know, or a famous person you don't know, make sure the physical description of your character is dramatically different from that of the real person. In fact, this may become the justification for physical description that you might not otherwise include—simply to distinguish your physical character from anyone real.

And no, adding "any similarity to any persons living or dead is purely coincidental" to the copyright page will not help you in the slightest. Some writers I know have obtained signed waivers from people granting permission to be mentioned in a book, but even that may not be enough if the subject decides the portrait in your book is unflattering. The sad thing about litigation is that, even if you win, it will cost you a fortune. Better to not do anything that might land you in court in the first place.

There are a few exceptions. If you're writing historical fiction, you may want to include people who actually lived in your story. That's fine. The nice thing about dead people is that they can't sue, and no, their heirs can't sue on their behalf, though you may hear from history buffs who dislike what you did to their hero.

The safest course is always to use your imagination, remaining true to the people you have known and the experiences you've had without expressly drawing from them. Describe the character your story needs.

HIGHLIGHTS/EXERCISES

Highlights

1) Creating a character should involve more than physical description.

2) The best character descriptions have both an identifying and a defining aspect.

3) Let the reader supply details that don't matter.

4) Describe the impact your character has on others.

5) Physical description is not as important as other descriptive details that bring the character to life.

6) Don't base your characters on real people you know or famous people you don't know.

Red Sneaker Exercises

1) Make a list of the five most important characters in your work-in-progress. For each, see if you can identify a dominant or defining trait. Ask yourself: if I could only tell the reader one thing about this character, what would it be? Avoid overt telling and search for details that indicate without explicating. Can you do it? Now, how can you introduce this information early enough for the reader to understand its import? And how much description can you now cut because it isn't needed anymore?

2) Does it matter what this character looks like? Pick a scene from your work-in-progress and consider the subsidiary characters, the ones who aren't leads but have some plot function to fulfill. If it doesn't matter what they look like, what more informative detail could you give the reader when they appear in the book? Could you describe how others react to them? Could you suggest some tension or conflict? Could you give the reader some reason to trust or disbelieve them?

3) Does a character in your story have a deep dark secret? (If this is a mystery, there may be many.) How can you use description to hint at this secret without giving it away? When the secret is revealed, you want your reader to have an "Aha!" moment, the sense that something was in front of them all along but they didn't see it—as opposed to feeling that something important has come completely out of left field, which makes readers less likely to accept it.

6

DESCRIPTION THAT SHOWS BUT DOESN'T TELL

"Create a world in front of your readers where they can taste, smell, touch, hear, see, and move. Or else they are likely going to move on to another book."

— PAWAN MISHRA

In my book, *What Writers Need to Know*, I discussed the old writer adage, "Show, don't tell." This line gets passed around a great deal at writers' conferences, but often people find it confusing. Don't you have to tell the reader what's going on, at least some of the time? Of course. But when it comes to characters' emotions, what's stirring on the inside, you show rather than tell.

Years ago, in *Mystery and Manners*, Flannery O'Conner, wrote that, "Fiction writing is very seldom a matter of saying things; it is a matter of showing things." To be sure, she doesn't say that there can never be any showing—but she makes it clear that it should be the exception, not the rule.

How do you show without telling? Through description.

"Show, don't tell" means you indicate the character's emotional state without directly feeding it to the reader.

SHOWING AND TELLING

WELL-WRITTEN DESCRIPTION CAN BE ONE OF THE MOST beautiful, most memorable, and most elegant ways of showing, of making something evident to the reader without pounding them on the head with it. Restraint may be necessary. This is not an opportunity to get too prosy, and excess never improved a book, especially in the realm of popular fiction. But when you are trying to communicate an emotion, a feeling, an ambiance, a mood, or a tone—well-crafted description may allow you to do it without express telling.

Description can provide an elegant means of showing without telling.

Let me give you an example. You're writing a party scene and you want to make it clear the party was a success. In your first draft, you might write:

EVERYONE HAD A LOVELY TIME AT THE PARTY.

IN YOUR SECOND DRAFT, HOWEVER, YOU REALIZE THAT THIS IS A BIT thin, and worse, it's all telling, and a result, has no emotional punch. Remember the party scene that Charles Dickens (him again) wrote for *A Christmas Carol*? We think of Scrooge as a miserly workaholic, but The Ghost of Christmas Past helps him remember his former employer Fezziwig, who knew how to celebrate Christmas. He ordered everyone "No more work tonight. Christmas Eve, Dick. Christmas, Ebenezer! Let's have the shutters up."

The description leaves no doubt that Fezziwig's party is a success.

WHEN THIS RESULT WAS BROUGHT ABOUT, OLD FEZZIWIG, CLAPPING his hands to stop the dance, cried out, "Well done!" and the fiddler plunged his hot face into a pot of porter, especially provided for that purpose.

THIS COMES AFTER DICKENS HAS DESCRIBED THE DANCING AND merrymaking in full though not excessive detail. There's lots of action, lots of emotion, and at no point does it feel like description. It does a fine job of "showing," providing the emotional content crucial to this story, as Scrooge gradually realizes how much he has given up in his dogged pursuit of money.

Let me give you one more example, this time from my favorite story, "Ylla," from my favorite book, *The Martian Chronicles*. This story revolves around a married couple—but they're Martians, with yellow coin eyes and musical voices. Judging from their behavior, they are no different from human couples who find, after the passage of time, that the magic has gone out of the relationship. But Bradbury never actually says that. Instead, he lets the reader discover it on their own.

First, Bradbury reminds you that Mr. and Mrs. K "were not old." Then he describes their life together as it once had been.

ONCE THEY HAD LIKED PAINTING PICTURES WITH CHEMICAL FIRE, swimming in the canals in the seasons when the wine trees filled them with green liquors, and talking into the dawn together by the blue phosphorous portraits in the speaking room.

. . .

THIS IS A BEAUTIFUL PIECE OF DESCRIPTION THAT, ONCE AGAIN, does not feel like description. It feels more like a flashback, though brief enough that no one minds. When you realize that they are not happy anymore, that their life today has lost the joy it once had—you are not surprised. Because the description is so finely crafted, because it seems exotic and unearthly and just enough without being too much, the reader feels the longing, the aching, the loss. Later in the story, when Mr. K takes extreme measures to protect his marriage—or the memory of the marriage that once was—the reader believes it, because Bradbury has done such a fine job of showing what they have lost.

REVEALING YOUR CHARACTER'S INNER FEELINGS

THERE ARE MANY SOUND REASONS TO ILLUMINATE YOUR character by showing rather than telling, even if you aren't persuaded by quotes from Flannery O'Conner or, for that matter, me. You have probably heard the expression, "Actions speak louder than words." It's true, not only in real life but in fiction. More than two thousand years ago, in the first-ever explication of what makes superior drama, *Poetics*, Aristotle wrote, "Action is character." Scholars debate this, but to me, that means you find out who someone really is not through what they say or think about themselves, but by observing what they do. How they conduct themselves. What choices they make. If you want the reader to get a handle on who your character truly is, you don't throw adjectives at them.

You show them. Through actions.

Let the reader discover your characters through their actions.

Atticus Finch shows who he is when he stands up to the lynch mob and prevents them from hauling Jim out of the jail. Daisy Buchanan shows who she is when she allows Gatsby to take the rap for her hit-and-run. Reverend Dimmesdale shows who he is when he allows Hester to take all the flack for her illegitimate child, while he pretends to be pious and pure. Hawthorne didn't have to tell you the man was a loser. You got there on your own when you read about his actions.

Are there other ways you can use description to reveal emotions without telling? Let me take the list in *What Writers Need to Know* and retool it to focus on description:

Body language indicates character emotions without telling.

We all know the body indicates emotions (often far better than words). That's why we have our characters smile, shrug, inhale, whisper, etc. The problem is that a little of that goes a long way, it soon becomes repetitive, and some body-language indicators are so obvious that it is basically telling. I do my best to eliminate stock phrases like "Ben took a deep breath" or "Daniel grinned" because they're really more space-fillers than they are informative.

An over- or underreaction suggests something unspoken lies beneath the surface.

When someone suddenly flies off the handle for no apparent reason, it usually indicates something is simmering inside. Ben Kincaid is shy and generally soft-spoken, so on those rare occasions when he suddenly erupts, or has any extreme emotion—you know something is bothering him. The same is true for an unnatural underreaction. Either way, it cues the reader that something unstated is troubling the character and encourages them to figure out what it is. Another mystery to solve, which always keeps readers turning pages.

Tics and tells often reveal what someone is thinking.

According to BB Thomas, my protagonist in *The Game Master*

(who won the World Series of Poker), everyone has a tell. The reader may not recognize the tell at first—but they will in time, and that will be a wonderful moment that will not only let them feel smart but will also inspire them to think you are a skilled writer. Ben Kincaid stuttered when he was worried or experienced some other suppressed emotion. Susan Pulaski (*Dark Eye*) drank. What's happening with your character? My advice: try to avoid the obvious—like averting eyes or clearing throats. Come up with something less on-the-nose, something readers may not immediately grasp, but will love when they do and will relish when it reoccurs—because they now know what it means, without being told.

Passive-aggressive responses indirectly indicate emotion.

Entire books have been written about passive-aggression, but the general idea is that someone superficially acquiesces, but does so in a way that reveals hostility. If you ask your partner if they want to go to the movies and they answer, "We could do that"—is that a "yes"? "Sure, if you want to" is similarly noncommittal. "You do whatever you want. You always do" is edging closer to plain aggression and seems a bit too obvious. This is another reason to write "off-the-nose" dialogue, which as I explained in *Dynamic Dialogue*, is often the most interesting to read.

What is paramount is that you give the reader an opportunity to connect to your main character. When readers identify, even with a character completely unlike themselves—that's when you know you've writen something terrific.

Don't Tell What You've Already Shown

AT THIS POINT, I HOPE YOU'RE SEEING WHY IT IS NOT ONLY MORE artistic but more strategic to show rather than tell. Trust the reader. Let the reader feel smart. Let them tease out the truth—which shouldn't be all that difficult if you've written it well. As even Flannery O'Connor allowed, there may be a few circumstances when you need to simply suck it up and tell.

But there is one instance when you should never tell.

Never tell readers what you've already shown them.

I see this problem in my small-group retreats all the time. Students do a fine job of describing something, of showing the character's emotional state without telling. But they feel insecure about it...so they add a conclusory sentence that spells out what they hinted at before.

That's a sentence I always cut.

The worst place to see this is at the end of a story or novel. Too often, writers seem to write the perfect clever subtle ending...and then write one sentence more. Or one paragraph more. Something tacked on that doesn't need to be there. It's like the insecure writer has jumped onto the page and started waving his hands, shouting, "Did you get it? I wanted to make sure you got it!"

Don't do that.

Have faith in your work. Let enough be enough.

This may be a good reason to use beta readers. Let the test audience tell you if your message is being conveyed, if the reader is getting what you want them to get. My bet is that most of the time, you'll find they did, and the offending explicatory passage can be struck, dismembered, and interred. Imagine if Dickens had ended his passage describing Fezziwig's celebration by saying, "A good time was had by one and all." Wouldn't that suck the joy out of it? Imagine if Bradbury had ended with, "They were deeply in love with one another once, but not so much anymore." Meh.

Let your work stand on its own. Even if there are a few speed-readers who miss the point, there will be far more who appreciate the fact that you wrote with art and craft and subtlety. So strike those unneeded conclusory summations.

Deciding when to show rather than tell, deciding how much is enough, deciding when to describe and how long to do it, are all matters that in time, with experience, will become instinctive to you, especially when you are revising, refining, and perfecting your words. You won't get there overnight. A common adage in the writing world is, "Every writer has a million words of crap to get out before you get to the good stuff." But if you persevere, you will get to the good stuff, or more specifically, you will acquire skills that allow you to judge when you've given the reader enough information to understand your characters, who they are and what they're feeling, without cramming it down their throats. That's when those scenes and characters will spring to life on the page, satisfying the reader and giving you the writing career you want.

HIGHLIGHTS/EXERCISES

Highlights

1) "Show, don't tell" means you indicate the character's emotional state without directly feeding it to the reader.

2) Description can provide a beautiful approach to showing without telling.

3) Let the reader discover your characters through their actions.

4) Body language indicates character emotions without telling.

5) An over- or underreaction suggests something unspoken lies beneath the surface.

6) Tics and tells often reveal what someone is thinking.

7) Passive-aggressive responses indirectly indicate emotion.

8) Never tell the reader what you've already shown.

9) Have faith in your work. Let enough be enough.

Red Sneaker Exercises

1) Find a chapter in your work-in-progress, or if you don't have one, a book you're reading, in which the lead character interacts with someone else. Can you tell what the character's emotional state is? How do you know? Is it shown or told? Does the dialogue have adverbs and other tells indicating emotion? Could you rewrite the passage to eliminate them?

2) Do you have a tendency to summarize paragraphs to make sure the reader got the point? We were taught in school to write topic sentences (at least in nonfiction), but no one needs topic conclusions. If you have a tendency to write one sentence too many, scour your manuscript for them—and take them out. If necessary, strengthen the description, but eliminate the telling.

3) Can you describe an important scene without telling? Describe the boy at the principal's office and his nervousness without saying he's nervous. Describe the gaiety at a party without saying the attendees are merry. Show a couple who have fallen out of love with one another without being on-the-nose about it.

7

DESCRIPTION TRAPS

"When you rewrite, your main job is taking out all the things that are *not* in the story."

— STEPHEN KING

After several chapters of instruction on what to do when describing, you're probably not surprised to encounter a chapter about what *not* to do when describing. Some of these have already been indicated, explicitly or implicitly. Replace telling adjectives and adverbs with more specific and informative nouns and verbs. Avoid Tom Swiftie dialogue tags. Don't describe what you've already implied. Don't rely excessively on visual description. But here are a few I haven't discussed, or haven't discussed in sufficient detail.

DITCHING THE TOO-FAMILIAR

. . .

WHEN I DISCUSSED FIGURATIVE LANGUAGE, AND SPECIFICALLY metaphor, I urged you to create your own to describe a situation without actually describing it. To be less literal and more creative. This was just a small step toward a larger rule—avoid cliché. Trite aphorisms can become an unenlightening shorthand for the lazy writer.

Avoid cliché whenever possible. And it's always possible.

Of course it's easier to rely on a descriptive phrase you've heard many times before. It's simpler to say someone was "mad as a wet hen" or "honest as the day is long" or "sweet as molasses." And these well-worn phrases have the advantage of being immediately understood by readers—because they've also heard them many times before. But that doesn't make it good writing. Even if you claim to not care about the artistry of your work, bear in mind that, although these phrases are understood by the reader, they are still not interesting. They do not conjure intriguing images in the reader's mind. They do not bring a scene to life. They are the metaphoric equivalent of telling sentences like "Bertha was sad" because they have so little vigor or originality.

Next time you're tempted to use a cliché in your writing—or perhaps when you're revising and spot one in your early draft— take a moment to see if you can invent something fresher. This might be a good time to get up and move, walk around the block, take the dogs for a spin. Get some blood flowing. Recall that the operative word in the phrase "creative writing" is "creative." Think of a substitute image. Wet hens aren't really mad, they're just wet and they don't like being wet. The image works because a wet hen moves fast and looks unhappy. Can you come up with another image that conveys the same impression? Give it a few moments and I'll bet you can. Your prose will be much more energetic because you didn't settle for the obvious.

AVOID POINTED DESCRIPTIONS

. . .

IN *THINKING THEME*, I WROTE ABOUT THE IMPORTANCE OF HAVING something to write about—and also about not pounding readers over the head with it. Theme should emerge in a gradual and understated way. There should never be a character, or an offscreen narrator, who announces "what the story is all about." My influence here is John Gardner, who likened theme to a debate topic. Here's something important we should all dwell upon, but I'm not going to tell you what to think. Remember the words of André Gide: "Often with good sentiments we produce bad literature."

Description is not your opening to get preachy.

Some writers have been known to incorporate overt messages in their descriptions, and this is almost always a mistake. Few readers pick up novels hoping for a sermon. Confirmation bias makes us all more receptive to messages that support our pre-existing beliefs, but too much didacticism leaves readers feeling dismayed. Readers want to be entertained. That does not mean your story can't have anything to say. It does mean you shouldn't let it overwhelm your story or shape your descriptions.

My book *Challengers of the Dust* is a historical novel set in Oklahoma during the Dust Bowl. A grandfather tells his wayward grandson about an adventure from his youth—possibly enhanced by the passage of time and his desire to tell a lively story. The tale is told in the manner of a fable—you can believe as much of it as you like or none at all. It becomes evident, as the book proceeds, that these adventures had an impact on the grandfather, and he wants his grandson to absorb the same lessons. The grandfather learned tolerance after spending time with all sorts of people—black, white, rich, poor, gay, homeless. But he never says that. The reader may see the change in him, but no one spells it out explicitly.

In one of my favorite scenes in the book, the protagonist,

George, visits the home of the wealthiest citizen in town, the doctor, the man who has a greenhouse blooming rare orchids— while most of the people in town are starving to death. Do I tell you what to think of this man? No. Does George tell the reader what he thinks of this man? No.

It isn't necessary. The description of the doctor's huge home, the upholstered furniture, the servants, his repressed wife and daughter, the monumental amount of time and money poured into flowers that only bloom for an hour, is more than enough. The reader absorbs what they need to know from the description, which creeps up on them, detail by detail, until the reader has a full understanding of who this doctor is. But the reader is never told anything. Only shown.

Don't Let Your Feelings Get Away From You

You already know what I think of description that goes on too long and provides more detail than the reader actually needs. You know I don't like description that duplicates information the reader has already received. Some writers, particularly early writers, really want to describe. Some feel it's a requirement. Some simply like it. I've heard writers at my retreats say they feel description is what they do best. They may be sketchy on dialogue or action or character, but they love to describe.

That's a problem.

Don't let description become a distracting digression.

In the first place, if you think description is your strong suit, you may want to consider writing nonfiction rather than fiction. Description alone is not storytelling, and if you don't want to tell a story, making one up may be problematic. The other difficulty, of course, is that if writers love describing, they're likely to do too much of it. Sometimes people resent it when I suggest they should reduce or cut a descriptive passage, because that's what they think they do best.

Description cannot be your excuse for a meandering story.

Novels are narratives. Even in literary fiction, it is about storytelling. And while description can enhance a story, a long passage that wanders off the track and loses the narrative thread is unlikely to improve the quality of your book. Rarely if ever have I brought my characters to a new location that could not be described adequately in a paragraph. Maybe less, depending upon how familiar that location is likely to be to the reader.

If you outlined your novel, you likely made a note of the location—but the majority of what you wrote was about what happens and who it happens to, right? Sure, the characters have to be somewhere when they interact, but that isn't the most important part of the chapter and never should be. For some books, the exotic location is part of the appeal, and of course, many writers think setting is so important it becomes a character (more on that in the next chapter). But you make that happen through the eyes and ears of your characters without killing the story. You integrate the description rather than dumping on the reader.

If you think you're on a roll, spilling out some of the best descriptive work you've done in your life, I don't want to be the one who kills the buzz. Let it roll. But later, when you're revising, remember—less is more. How much of that prose, brilliant though it may be, do you really need? There is another aphorism in the writing world that's relevant here—Kill your darlings. Sometimes, much as you love what you've written, it still needs to be eliminated, because it isn't making the overall book better. Fiction is about far more than pretty words. You have to consider the big picture.

Kill your darlings.

One last word. If you find yourself cutting a big portion of prose, be it description or something else, save it in a separate file. There's no reason to trash it just because you removed it from your work-in-progress, and saving it may ease the pain of cutting. Who knows—that saved passage may turn out to be just what you need in some later effort. My friend Steve Berry talks about a long action sequence he eliminated from one of his early books, because the overall book was simply too long. But he managed to use that passage, with some minor revisions, in a later book, which saved him a lot of time and trouble.

Here's a story for those of you who, like me, love musicals. Jerome Kern and the pre-Rogers Oscar Hammerstein were putting together *Show Boat*, arguably the first musical with a mature plot and songs that advanced the story. They knew they had something special. But to balance the serious story, at one point, they needed a comic song to lighten the mood. The song Hammerstein wrote wasn't working. Comedy wasn't his strong suit at that point and he knew it. Worse, they needed a song fast because opening night was creeping up on them. Hammerstein remembered a song ("Bill") with lyrics by the masterful P.G. Wodehouse that had been cut from a different show and suggested that they get permission to use it in *Show Boat*. Follow that? Hammerstein suggested they use the work of a different lyricist—because he knew it was what the show needed. He put the production ahead of his own ego.

And that's why *Show Boat* became a classic.

Focus on the big picture. Make the overall book as good as it can be.

In the Appendices, I'm attaching a list of potential description problems that you should be vigilant about avoiding—a checklist for clutter. In this respect, description is no different from any other aspect of writing. Ray Bradbury divided writing into two phases, "throwing up and cleaning up."

There's enormous truth there. Writing a book is an ongoing process of separating what works from what doesn't. First you get your story down on paper in the rawest form possible. You tell the story. After that, you start thinking about how *best* to tell the story. Almost inevitably, while you may make some additions during revision, you will do more cutting. Eliminating the unnecessary. Separating the wheat from the chaff. It's part of the process. And nowhere more so than with description.

HIGHLIGHTS/EXERCISES

Highlights

1) Avoid cliché whenever possible. And it's always possible.

2) Description is not your chance to get preachy.

3) Don't let description become a distracting digression.

4) Description cannot be your excuse for a meandering story.

5) Kill your darlings.

6) Focus on the big picture. Make the overall book as good as it can be.

Red Sneaker Exercises

1) Take a coldhearted professional approach to any description in your story that goes on longer than two sentences. Exercise your surgical skills. What does the third sentence contribute that is

not contained in the first two? Could you rewrite this and pare it down to two sentences—and I don't mean two sentences with multiple subordinate clauses inserted to cram in more information. I mean two concise sentences that tell readers what they need to know.

2) Any time you find yourself smiling at a turn of phrase you've composed, be afraid. Anytime you find yourself saying your words out loud, thinking about how nice they will sound when you read them to an audience, be wary. You may be letting your love of language and writing overcome your authorial judgment.

8

FINDING THE TIME AND PLACE

"The writer operates at a peculiar crossroads where time and place and eternity somehow meet. His problem is to find that location."

— FLANNERY O'CONNOR

Setting is not the same as description, but they are closely enough related that I thought a chapter on setting might be appropriate. To be sure, describing your setting is the most common way to establish it, though as we have discussed, opening your book with long-winded descriptions of the landscape or the weather may not be the most rip-snorting way to kick off a story. Still, it makes sense to consider setting while you have all these first-rate principles of description in your head.

In recent years, I've heard an increasing number of writers, sometimes successful literary folk, talking about how "setting is a character" in their work. I think what they're saying, at least most of the time, is that setting is important. Setting must be brought to life. If you give the reader a strong sense of location in time and space, it will make the book better. I have no problem with that. But running around telling newbie writers that "setting is a character" creates confusion without explaining anything or providing useful guidance. Like too much writing instruction out there, it obfuscates rather than explicates. So for the purposes of this book, let's agree that setting is important and leave it at that.

SETTING MATTERS

TO BE SURE, THIS IS EASIER IN SOME BOOKS THAN IN OTHERS. YOU may be thinking that setting has two dimensions—when and where—but it actually has three—when, where, and *how long*. The other, less-obvious component of setting is what timespan your book encompasses, and in many cases, this can be the most important of the three.

Most books, particularly in popular fiction, take place over a relatively brief period of time. This may harken back to Aristotle's directives about unity of time. A story unfolding over a relatively brief period seems to have more urgency than one unspooled over centuries. You will generate more tension by having a character say something like, "Scotty, we need warp drive in three minutes or we're all dead" than you'll get from, "You know, we really ought to do something about this sometime."

You can probably think of exceptions. Isaac Asimov's wonderful Foundation series spans decades, but there's still a great deal of tension as you wait to discover whether Hari Seldon's predictions—based upon his psychohistory—will be correct. Many novels—*David Copperfield* and *Slaughterhouse-Five*, for two obvious though extremely different examples—have encompassed a protagonist's entire life, or at least many decades of it. *A Christmas Carol* gives us scenes from many years of Scrooge's life—even though the story takes place in about twelve hours stretching from Christmas Eve to Christmas morning. For your first novel, however, you may find it easier to limit your story to a more manageable period of time.

You should locate the story for readers by giving them a strong sense of time and place.

If you set your first novel in your own hometown, as so many have done, you have some obvious advantages. No research, right? You know this place inside out. The drawback is that convenience doesn't always equal excellence. You want the location that will be best for the story you're writing, not the one that's easiest to manage. You want a location that will interest readers, not bore them. Historical fiction will require extensive research if you hope to get the setting right. Science fiction set in some future time will require enormous amounts of imagination and world-building. You can do it, but don't kid yourself. Settings like this will be more challenging.

Find the setting that is perfect for the story you want to tell.

Creating an Internally Consistent World

Part of establishing your setting, particularly if it is an imaginative setting that doesn't actually exist, will be establishing the "rules." Fiction works best when your imaginary world has its own consistent laws. Otherwise, you run the risk of creating a world that seems to have been made up as you wrote along, inventing rules to suit your present authorial needs. You can still arrange the world as works best for you, but establish the rules early so the reader does not see the writer's hand in it.

Most horror stories, for instance, benefit from having rules. Vampires can't go out in the sunlight and must be invited into your home. Werewolves only appear when the moon is full and can be killed with silver bullets. Invisible people always go bonkers. None of this really makes any sense, but if you establish the rules up front, it gives the setting a dimension of "reality" that it might not otherwise have.

Interestingly, when Stephanie Meyer created her fictional universe for the Twilight saga, she upended many of the traditional rules for fictional vampires—but created other rules to take their place. She probably realized early on that it would be hard to show vampires in high school if they couldn't go out in the sun, so that rule was amended. They can go out, in the frequently overcast Forks, Washington, and they won't burst into flames. They just sparkle. Furthermore, they are not monsters. They can acquire blood from non-human sources. And their society has laws, even a governing body, that creates all kinds of problems, especially when Edward starts breaking the rules. Meyer's world may not be real, but it is internally consistent, which is one reason so many readers found it appealing.

Create an internally consistent world.

SETTING THAT HEIGHTENS THE DRAMA

JOHN STEINBECK'S *EAST OF EDEN* FAMOUSLY OPENS WITH A description of Salinas County. Probably not how I would've done it, but since Steinbeck won the Nobel Prize, I won't argue about it. The description is beautifully written, doesn't go too long, and soon brings us to our protagonist, who says, "I remember my childhood names for grasses and secret flowers." So this passage, while establishing the setting, has also introduced our narrator and set a nostalgic tone for the story. This story is something that happened in the past, something the narrator has still not gotten over, which may be why he is telling the story. He also talks about what trees and seasons smelled like, because as we already discussed, the sense of smell is linked to recollection. "The memory of odors is very rich."

Use setting to establish tone, mood, or meaning.

In my novel *Dark Eye*, I violated every principle I had established in the Ben Kincaid novels. I had a new, grittier, female protagonist, Susan Pulaski, and she spoke directly to the reader. I allowed the book to open with a descriptive passage portraying a seedy Vegas bar. This does establish the setting—but also does much more. It is filled with tension and it introduces the lead character, who you soon realize has some serious problems. At the end of the passage, she makes a terrible mistake which calls into question her ability to perceive, much less describe. Readers obtain more than location—they understand that their first-person narrator is damaged, unreliable, and everything she said may be wrong.

There are some instances when it is more legit to claim that your setting is a character. I was mesmerized years ago by Robert Altman's film *Nashville*. Note the title. Not a person but a place. The movie has a large ensemble cast interacting with one another, people from all walks of life, and it culminates with a tragic event. Why so many characters? Because Altman is using them to give viewers a sense of the city, the true subject. At the end, after the assassination, one of the characters says, "This is Nashville, not Dallas." But the clear suggestion is that the two cities are not all that different from one another, that people are people, no matter where they're located.

Setting can be used to amplify a theme, especially in the most overtly didactic books. Certainly this is what Harriet Beecher Stowe did in *Uncle Tom's Cabin*, a novel that changed American history. Stowe rocked the world by portraying the horrors of slavery. But there is little preaching in the story. It's a thriller, and the plot rarely lags. The power comes from the description and the setting. When readers were exposed to the everyday life of the slave—long hours, abuse, horrible living conditions, families torn apart—they understood the evils of slavery in a way that took it out of the abstract and into the immediate. Upton Sinclair did much the same in *The Jungle*, a novel that wrought profound changes to the meat-packing industry, after Sinclair described that setting in gruesome detail. You may choose to be subtler in your work, but you can still use your setting to make a point.

YOU DON'T HAVE TO REALLY LIVE THERE

YOU CAN BRING TO LIFE A SETTING THAT IS NOT ONLY UNFAMILIAR to you, but to your readers, but it will be a challenge. Here are some guiding principles:

Make your characters believe in this world.

Focus on the humans living in this world.

Use technical terms, facts, and pseudo-facts to create a sense of reality.

Establish your credentials.

Eliminate every apparent reason why this couldn't happen.

Remember that setting and description should move the book forward (not slow it down).

Create a world readers want to visit.

What are some of the most unusual fictional worlds you've visited? Science fiction and fantasy are more popular now than ever before. SF and superheroes dominate the cineplex. What makes those worlds convincing? What makes people believe in them enough to be absorbed by the drama?

Michael Crichton's *Jurassic Park* was a huge bestseller, and no one was surprised when Steven Spielberg decided it should be a movie. To an earlier generation, the "high concept" of this book would have seemed preposterous. Dinosaurs brought to life? And assembled in a theme park so people can hang out with the most dangerous creatures to ever walk the face of the earth? Ridiculous.

So how did Crichton and Spielberg sell the concept? By using the principles I discussed in *Powerful Premise*. First, let's start with the author. Crichton had a reputation for being a scientist, so he had the all-important credibility going into the project. (In reality, Crichton finished medical school, never did rotations, never practiced, and certainly was never a research scientist. But like all good writers, he took what he had and made the most of it.) The creation of the park, though fictional, has grains of recognizable truth in it. The book takes deep dives into scientific jargon. I suspect most readers followed little of that, but its presence added more credibility, gave it a greater sense of scientific feasibility.

And there are recognizable elements, even for non-scientists. The park creators used DNA—well, ok, I've heard of that. The dinos are clones—sure, like that sheep in England. They got dino DNA from mosquitos. Everyone knows mosquitos suck blood, and blood has DNA, and if a mosquito got trapped in amber, the DNA might be preserved millions of years later. (Extremely doubtful, actually, but at this point, aren't you more than willing to go along with it?) The characters in the story all believe it's possible, and most of the time, don't even act like it's that complicated.

Pulling off an achievement like this requires you to do your homework, even if you're in your specialty field. If you're going to write hard science fiction, you need to get up to snuff on the science. If you're going to write historical fiction, you need to know the era inside out. This is part of establishing the credibility. As soon as a reader catches an error or anachronism—or something they think is—they've been yanked out of the story, probably never to return. Some readers love to catch boo-boos. It makes them feel superior, even if, as it turns out, they were wrong. You can't protect yourself from all criticism. But you can protect yourself from negative comments arising from your mistakes—by doing the necessary background work.

There is one more factor that must be considered here—desirability. If the fictional setting you're creating is attractive, a place where readers would like to spend some time, they are much more likely to share your fantasy. Who wouldn't want to see actual dinosaurs? People flock to Disney World and Universal Studios to see animatronic recreations. Wouldn't you go see the real deal? I know I would. I don't care if the dinos get loose (as they always seem to do). I'm in.

Crichton created a fantasy setting so appealing that readers were more than willing to suspend belief and travel with him.

The clear break from reality can be part of a setting's appeal.

The same could probably be said of Tolkien's Middle Earth, and for younger readers, C.S. Lewis' Narnia. Despite the enormous danger lurking around each and every corner, Frodo's world seems immensely appealing. Fun. Exciting, filled with orcs, and elves, and sorcerers. I'd go on a quest there, wouldn't you? I'd even wear the ring, and we all know where that leads. Who cares? You can't pass on a great adventure.

I never imagined I would want to spend five hundred pages with a bunch of rabbits, but *Watership Down* was a terrific adventure story, set in a fully imagined animal world with not only rules but a complex rabbit society that made internal sense. And millions of readers worldwide thrilled to the imaginary world of creatures and sorcerers—and a governing Ministry of Magic—created by J.K. Rowling.

Let's revisit Ray Bradbury's *The Martian Chronicles*. It's worth noting that Bradbury wrote most of the stories in the book in the 1950s. By that time, we already knew that the Martian "canals" weren't really canals and that there was no sign of anything resembling humanoid life on the planet. Bradbury could have set these stories on another planet. He deliberately chose to set them on Mars even though it was scientifically impossible. Part of that may have been his nostalgia for the great Edgar Rice Burroughs stories set on Mars (that is, Barsoom). But by deliberately setting these stories in a place where they could not happen, he signaled his readers that these stories were not science fiction and should not be taken that way. These were not visions of the future. They were metaphors. They had nothing to say about technology but everything to say about humanity, its foibles, its self-destructive tendencies, and its survival instincts, all wrapped in poetic prose that enhanced the metaphors.

LARGE DETAILS AND SMALL

YOUR NEXT BOOK MAY TAKE PLACE IN A FAMILIAR LOCATION THAT requires little defining—but that doesn't mean you shouldn't work to bring it to life. Just don't do it with long stretches of description telling readers what they likely already know. Try to provide insight, not geography. Give the reader a sense of the people, through dialogue and interaction. Give them a sense of the inherent conflicts. Often small details are the most telling—a word choice, a t-shirt choice, a drink order, a weekend recreation. Give the reader the big picture and the small, the macro and the micro, the aerial view and the closeup. Give them a sense that this location was not chosen at random, but rather, was chosen because it is the perfect place to tell that story. If you do your job right, you'll have readers packing their bags to join you. Metaphorically.

Use both large and small details to create a thoroughly developed setting.

Description and setting can be challenging, even if you're doing both in a minimalistic way. But what about writing was ever easy? Don't worry—you can handle it. Bring your setting to life—but also remember that what readers are likely to remember most are your characters and the situations you put them in. I've received a lot of mail from readers over the years—but I've never once had anyone complain that I didn't describe enough or provide sufficient detail about the setting. So don't let these concerns overwhelm you. Instead, put your characters in a fully realized world filled with intrigue and possibility. Let description and setting become, not obstacles, but stepping stones on your path to success.

HIGHLIGHTS/EXERCISES

Highlights

1) You should locate the story for readers by giving them a strong sense of time and place.

2) Find the setting that is perfect for the story you want to tell.

3) Create an internally consistent world.

4) Use setting to establish tone, mood, or meaning.

5) Make your characters believe in this world.

6) Focus on the humans living in this world.

7) Use technical terms, facts, and pseudo-facts to create a sense of reality.

8) Establish your credentials.

9) Eliminate every apparent reason why this couldn't happen.

10) Remember that setting and description should move the book forward (not slow it down).

11) Create a world readers want to visit.

12) The clear break from reality can be part of a setting's appeal.

13) Use both large and small details to create a thoroughly developed setting.

Red Sneaker Exercises

1) Describe the setting for your work-in-progress or the book you're thinking about writing. No page limitations or requirements—write as much or as little as comes to mind. When you're finished, take a hard look at what you've written. How much of it would really help the reader grasp the setting? How much is redundant? Are there small details that would allow you to indicate aspects of the setting without spelling it out? Those are the keepers. Now think about how you can integrate this information without appearing to describe. If you haven't started writing yet, plant these keeper details in your outline so you will remember to insert them where appropriate, not gratuitously, but in the context of the story you're telling.

2) Can you use dialogue to establish your setting? And just to make this more challenging, can you do it without resorting to dialect and phonetic spellings that tend to slow down the read? Often the choice of word, the level of vocabulary, and the way sentences are constructed, can provide more information than dialect.

3) Are there ways to immerse yourself in your setting, even if it doesn't exist (or doesn't exist anymore)? You know a convincing historical setting will require more than reading a Wikipedia article or two. Your research must be extensive. Similarly, you may not be able to travel to another planet, but is there any place like it you could visit? Is it a desert world (as in *Dune*) or an ice world (like Krypton)? Where could you travel that might allow you to acquire some interesting details you could transplant to your fictional world?

4) Are there habits or rituals you could use to bring an environment to life? Many lawyers like to play golf. Some doctors like to hunt. Teachers like pub quizzes. Office workers often go to a bar together on Friday night. What rituals could you portray that might help create a vivid image of the world in which your characters live?

5) Who will you have beta-read your manuscript when it's finished? You may consider choosing someone who knows the setting and can comment on whether it comes alive in your book. Better yet, they may suggest details you could add to make the setting even more vivid.

APPENDIX A: CHECKLIST FOR DESCRIPTIVE CLUTTER

In his classic work, *On Writing Well*, William Zinsser calls clutter "the disease of American writing." He's right. And the tendency to cram in too much, more than is needed, is nowhere more prevalent than in description. Here's a convenient checklist to use when revising.

Avoid:

- Cliché
- Adjectives and Adverbs
- Repetition
- Preachiness
- Digression
- Unintentional misdirection
- Unneeded information or detail
- Uninformative character description
- Excessive visual description
- Excessive landscape description
- Excessive weather description

- Verbosity
- Dialogue tags
- Anything that cheats readers out of a chance to use their imaginations

APPENDIX B: THE RED SNEAKER
WRITER'S READING LIST

Appendix B: The Red Sneaker Writer's Reading List

The Chicago Manual of Style. 16th ed. Chicago: University of Chicago Press, 2010.

Cook, Vivian. *All in a Word: 100 Delightful Excursions into the Uses and Abuses of Words.* Brooklyn: Melville House, 2010.

Fowler, H.W. *Fowler's Modern English Usage.* 3rd ed. Rev. Ernest Gowers. N.Y. & Oxford: Oxford University Press, 2004.

Goldman, William. *Adventures in the Screen Trade: A Personal View of Hollywood and Screenwriting.* New York: Grand Central, 1989.

Hale, Constance. *Sin and Syntax: How to Create Wickedly Effective Prose.* New York: Broadway Books, 2001.

Hart, Jack. *A Writer's Coach: The Complete Guide to Writing Strategies That Work.* New York: Anchor Books, 2006.

Jones, Catherine Ann. *The Way of Story: The Craft and Soul of Writing.* Studio City: Michael Wiese Productions, 2007.

Klauser, Henriette Anne. *Writing on Both Sides of the Brain.* San Francisco: Harper & Row, 1987.

Maass, Donald. *The Fire in Fiction: Passion, Purpose, and Tech-*

niques to Make Your Novel Great. Cincinnati: Writers Digest Books, 2009.

Maass, Donald. *Writing the Breakout Novel: Insider Advice for Taking Your Fiction to the Next Level.* Cincinnati: Writers Digest Books, 2001.

Maass, Donald. *Writing 21st Century Fiction: High Impact Techniques for Exceptional Storytelling.* Cincinnati: Writers Digest Books, 2012.

O'Conner, Patricia T. *Woe Is I: The Grammarphobe's Guide to Better English in Plain English.* 2nd ed. New York: Riverhead Books, 2003.

O'Conner, Patricia T. *Origins of the Specious: Myths and Misconceptions of the English Language.* New York: Random House, 2009.

Strunk, William, Jr., and White, E.B. *The Elements of Style.* 4th ed. N.Y.: Macmillan, 2000.

Truss, Lynne. *Eats Shoots & Leaves: The Zero Tolerance Guide to Punctuation.* New York: Gotham Books, 2005.

Vogler, Christopher. *The Writer's Journey: Mythic Structure for Storytellers and Screenwriters.* Studio City: Michael Wiese Productions, 1992.

Zinsser, William. *On Writing Well: The Classic Guide to Writing Nonfiction.* 30th Anniv. Ed. New York: Harper Perennial, 2006.

ABOUT THE AUTHOR

William Bernhardt is the author of over fifty books, including *The Last Chance Lawyer* (*#1 Bestseller*), the historical novels *Challengers of the Dust* and *Nemesis*, two books of poetry, and the Red Sneaker books on fiction writing. In addition, Bernhardt founded the Red Sneaker Writers Center to mentor aspiring authors. The Center hosts an annual conference (WriterCon), small-group seminars, a newsletter, a phone app, and a bi-weekly podcast. He is also the owner of Balkan Press, which publishes poetry and fiction as well as the literary journal *Conclave*.

Bernhardt has received the Southern Writers Guild's Gold Medal Award, the Royden B. Davis Distinguished Author Award (University of Pennsylvania) and the H. Louise Cobb Distinguished Author Award (Oklahoma State), which is given "in recognition of an outstanding body of work that has profoundly influenced the way in which we understand ourselves and American society at large." In 2019, he received the Arrell Gibson Lifetime Achievement Award from the Oklahoma Center for the Book.

In addition Bernhardt has written plays, a musical (book and score), humor, children's stories, biography, and puzzles. He has edited two anthologies (*Legal Briefs* and *Natural Suspect*) as fundraisers for The Nature Conservancy and the Children's Legal Defense Fund. In his spare time, he has enjoyed surfing, digging for dinosaurs, trekking through the Himalayas, paragliding, scuba diving, caving, zip-lining over the canopy of the Costa Rican rain forest, and jumping out of an airplane at 10,000 feet.

In 2017, when Bernhardt delivered the keynote address at the

San Francisco Writers Conference, chairman Michael Larsen noted that in addition to penning novels, Bernhardt can "write a sonnet, play a sonata, plant a garden, try a lawsuit, teach a class, cook a gourmet meal, beat you at Scrabble, and work the *New York Times* crossword in under five minutes."

For more information
www.williambernhardt.com
wb@williambernhardt.com

AUTHOR'S NOTE

Watch for the next volume in the Red Sneaker Writers Book series.

Would you consider posting a review of this book online? I'd really appreciate it. I hope you'll also consider reading some of my fiction, including the Daniel Pike novels, starting with *The Last Chance Lawyer*.

Please consider attending WriterCon over Labor Day weekend in Oklahoma City. For more information, visit www.writercon.org. If you're interested in attending one of my small-group writing retreats, visit my webpage.

Need some feedback on your writing? Check out my Patreon page at https://www.patreon.com/willbern

I publish a free e-newsletter on a regular basis. The Red Sneaker Writers Newsletter is for writers and aspiring writers, filled with market and writing news. You can sign up at my website. There's also a bi-weekly Red Sneakers podcast, available everywhere you get podcasts.

For more information, please visit my website at http://www.williambernhardt.com. You can email me at willbern@gmail.com.

ALSO BY WILLIAM BERNHARDT

Murder One

Criminal Intent

Hate Crime

Death Row

Capitol Murder

Capitol Threat

Capitol Conspiracy

Capitol Offense

Capitol Betrayal

Justice Returns

Other Novels

The Last Chance Lawyer

The Code of Buddyhood

Dark Eye

The Midnight Before Christmas

Final Round

Double Jeopardy

Strip Search

Nemesis: The Final Case of Eliot Ness

The Game Master

Challengers of the Abyss

Poetry

The White Bird

The Ocean's Edge

Made in the USA
Coppell, TX
05 August 2020

32405475R00069